THE
Old Photographs
SERIES

AROUND
OTTERY ST MARY

Aerial view of Ottery St Mary Brickworks in 1931. The brickworks were situated one mile to the east of the town, off Chineway Road, and the production of hand-made bricks, tiles and, later, land drain pipes started in around 1820. In the early days power was supplied by steam engines, which were replaced by a 60hp single-cylinder Tangye engine in around 1924, when grinding mills and brick presses were also installed. At the same time the 10-chamber intermittent kiln was increased in size to make it a 20-chamber continous burning kiln. In the early 1930s a second Tangye diesel engine was put in to supply more power for further presses. After World War Two the digging of clay by hand was superseded by a mechanical excavator. The works generated its own electricity but went on to the mains supply around 1949. Hand moulding of bricks was gradually phased out until, in 1962, all production was by machine and weekly production was 125,000 bricks. The recession in the building trade led to production ceasing in August 1969.

THE
Old Photographs
SERIES
AROUND
OTTERY ST MARY

Compiled by
Gerald Gosling and Peter Harris

To Ron

With best Wishes

Peter Harris

CHALFORD

BATH • AUGUSTA • RENNES

The Chalford Publishing Company Limited
St Mary's Mill, Chalford, Stroud
Gloucestershire GL6 8NX

ISBN 07524 0030 4

Typesetting and origination by
Alan Sutton Limited
Printed in Great Britain

For Our Wives Pat and Violet

Ottery St Mary market in, unusually (it was generally held in The Square), Paternoster Row, in around 1909. Note the old police station, with porched door, behind.

Contents

Ottery St Mary Summer Carnival. This photograph was taken in Long Dogs Lane, c.1910. Left to right: Jess Hellier, Jack Veal, Cyril Godfrey.

Introduction

There is a place, Dear Native place!
Amid the meadows fair,
Between the hills, beside the stream,
Where blows the soft, light air.

This extract from the 'Old Ottery Song', composed by Bernard, Lord Coleridge, in 1910 for the Ottregian's Society, gives a flavour of Ottery St Mary in times past. This book is the story of Ottery St Mary and District told through old photographs.

Ottery St Mary is an ancient market town dating back to Saxon times. It is situated some twelve miles east of Exeter in the pleasant and fertile valley of the River Otter from which it takes its name. A dominant feature of the town is the Church of St Mary, a late 13th-century foundation which, together with Bishop Grandisson's college, was an important medieval establishment. Sadly, the college disappeared at the time of Henry VIII's Dissolution of the Monasteries, but Grandisson's church remains, a gem of ecclesiastical architecture. Another prominent building is the Factory, which opened in 1788 as a serge mill powered by the tumbling weir. The mill leat was in existence before the Norman Conquest to provide the power for corn mills.

As with many small towns, Ottery St Mary has changed greatly over the the years, particularly since World War Two. The self-sufficient, ancient market town based on local agriculture has now lost its market and has developed into a dormitory town to accommodate people working in Exeter and throughout East Devon. Nevertheless, Ottery St Mary retains many of its ancient traditions: the midsummer revels of Pixie Day; the arsonist's delight of

November 5th, with its flaming tar barrel rituals, and the handbells of Christmastide, with the nightwatchman announcing the Nativity of Our Lord.

I think there is a great fascination in old photographs for their portrayal of a bygone age. Too often in our hurry to grow up we neglect to ask our parents and grandparents the details of customs and traditions of their days. This book helps to fill some of the gaps. Gerald Gosling and Peter Harris are to be complemented on assembling and annotating such a wealth of material depicting the more recent past of Ottery St Mary and its neighbouring villages. These small villages contribute so much to the life of the community, as witness their present active and generous response to the appeal to raise funds towards equipping the new hospital.

F.G. 'Frank' Down,
Ottery St Mary, 1994

One

Ottery St Mary
The Place

Barrack Road, Ottery St Mary, c.1928. The round huts seen in the gardens were former World War One army huts given as garden sheds for the houses which were built in Barrack Road by Devon County Council for returning ex-servicemen.

Trumps Stores, Broad Street, Ottery St Mary, c.1908.

Trumps Stores, Broad Street, Ottery St Mary, c.1920. Now the site of the Victoria Wine shop, this was the Ottery branch of a grocery business founded in Sidmouth which enjoyed a reputation second to none in the area.

Yonder Street, Ottery St Mary, c.1905. Note the 'long service' bars on the postman's jacket pocket. The Co-op still occupies the same site today.

Broad Street, Ottery St Mary, c.1909. Most likely the crowd has gathered for Ottery Day. Part of Hake's shop (in the background) later became Trumps Stores, the other part Lovell's Garage. Today it is the local branch of the TSB. Bovett's bakery was later taken over by Reg Harris.

Kings Arms Hotel, Ottery St Mary, c.1950. A.C. Chivers' grocers shop on the left was formerly Mr Chandler's. Later it was a betting shop but it now stands empty.

Mill Street, Ottery St Mary, c.1912. The poles (with cross bars) on the edge of the pavements (a feature of the town at the time) were for securing the shop blinds. The Five Bells Inn in the far background was demolished to make way for the Canaan Way road entrance. Frank Williams' butchers is now a pet food shop. Luxton's, a china shop of some repute, is now a newsagents. Brocks on the left is now Cut & Curl (see p.37).

New Street, Ottery St Mary, c.1910. Note the muddy state of the road.

London Hotel (formerly Berry's London Inn), Ottery St Mary, c.1939. An air-raid shelter was built on this corner (of Silver and Gold Streets) during World War Two and stood there until demolished in around 1951.

Ottery St Mary station, c.1905. The 10.36, hauled by an Adams 02 tank locomotive, is just leaving the 'up' platform for Sidmouth Junction, where it connected with the Waterloo train.

Another Adams 02 tank engine entering Ottery St Mary station around 1905. Judging by the well-dressed appearance of the party of children, it is hauling a seaside excursion. This is borne out by the fact that it is a 'down' train, heading for either Sidmouth or Exmouth. The latter was always a popular destination for Ottery Sunday School outings.

Ottery St Mary railway station, c.1906.

Lamb Court, Ottery St Mary, c.1905. The thatched house has long since been demolished.

Ottery Day crowds in Silver Street, 1914. Manley's newsagents is on the right.

Brock's sweet shop, Mill Street, c.1905. Mrs Brock is seen with her two daughters, Gladys, later Mrs Grange (left), and Doris (Mrs Selley). The shop still sells sweets and still trades as Brock's. The post office, barely visible on the right, is also still there.

Broad Street, Ottery St Mary, c.1910. Hake was a well-known draper in East Devon; the shop is now shared between the TSB and Gribble, Booth & Taylor, the estate agents. Huxtables, in the background, now the Kitchen Shop, sold boots made on the premises.

Paternoster Row, Ottery St Mary, c.1910.

Cornhill, Ottery St Mary, 1905. Ottery's church was unusually lucky, the handsome railings seen here surviving the salvage drives of World War Two, which saw so many railings vanished for ever.

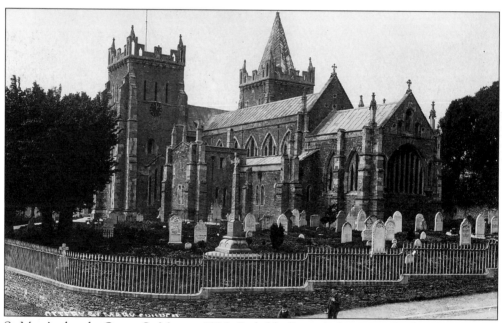

St Mary's church, Ottery St Mary, c.1926. Probably Devon's finest parish church, although some might, with good reason, advance the claims of Tiverton, Crediton or even Colyton. St Mary's has had thousands of words written about it. Let it be sufficient here to stay within the confines of editorial restraint and call it the town's 'Crowning Glory'.

Ottery St Mary Co-op in Yonder Street, c.1907. Billy Hansford's smithy is next door.

Raleigh House, Mill Street, Ottery St Mary, c.1905. The thatched house, the next two houses to its right and the Five Bells (see p.12) were demolished to make way for the Canaan Way road. The Wesleyan chapel is on the right.

Victoria Terrace, Mill Street, Ottery St Mary (c.1925), was built in 1909.

Broad Street and Market Place, Ottery St Mary, c.1946. A lorry belonging to Sercombe, the Exeter wholesale fruit merchants, has shed a load of plums. Cyril Bond, on the right, has come out of Trumps Stores to watch. Lovells shop later became Lovells Garage and moved to The Brook, these premises becoming the local branch of the TSB and the estate agents Gribble, Booth & Taylor.

Gosford Bridge and the level crossing house, c.1925.

Mill Stream and Cadhay Farm, Ottery St Mary, c.1910. The railings on the side of the road have been replaced.

Cadhay Road, looking towards Ottery St Mary, c.1930.

Broad Street, Ottery St Mary, c.1938. Billy Lee's garage is on the right. Next is Badcock's chemists shop. Mr W.D. Badcock produced and sold many of the early postcards which have been used in this book.

Silver Street, Ottery St Mary, c.1906. Manley News is now the National Westminster Bank, the Devon & Cornwall Bank is now Lloyds.

The Youth Hostel (c.1935), which was pulled down between 1958 and 1965 to make way for housing.

Yonder Street, Ottery St Mary, c.1903. Note the old basket pram on the right.

Ottery St Mary Cottage Hospital, c.1916. The hospital was largely the inspiration of Miss Isabella Elizabeth Elliot, who purchased the site in Lamb's Court (off Cornhill) where it opened in 1870 in Paxford House, next door to the present building which was erected and opened as the cottage hospital in 1882. The hospital was under the personal supervision of Miss Elliott for over twenty-two years, during which time she personally funded the project. Following the move to adjoining land in 1882, the new hospital had 'large airy wards and every hospital convenience'.

Prince William Inn the Plume of Feathers) in Yonder Street, looking towards Chineway, c.1902. Last orders were called on Thursday 9 June 1994 and the building demolished so that the site could be cleared for the building of foureeen houses

The Tuck Shop, seen here in around 1930, was at St Saviour's Bridge, Ottery St Mary (conveniently situated on the way to the King's School). It was an old disused railway carriage and was run by Mrs Lathrop, whose husband ran the gas works in the background.

The Chanter's House, Ottery St Mary, c.1912. The chanter, who was responsible for leading the singing in divine services during the time of the collegiate church at Ottery St Mary, lived here. It was renamed Heath's Court upon being purchased in 1685 by Thomas Heath. Purchased by James Coleridge in 1796, it has remained in that family's possession ever since, changing its name back to Chanter's House in the late 19th century.

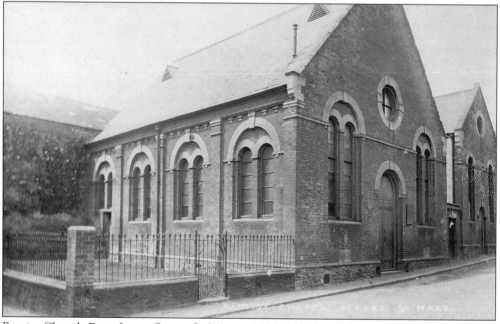

Baptist Chapel, Batts Lane, Ottery St Mary, c.1920. This housed the fire station (before its move to the Land of Canaan) after World War Two.

Basten's Dairy, Mill Street, Ottery St Mary, c.1905. This is now housing.

Stafford House, Cornhill, Ottery St Mary, seen her in around 1959, was built in 1760 and is reputed to be named after Lord Henry Stafford, Earl of Wiltshire.

Mill Street, Ottery St Mary, looking towards The Square, c.1904.

Pixies Parlour, Ottery St Mary, where Samuel Taylor Coleridge is said to have written some of his poetry. Seen here in around 1930, it is reputed to have been the home of the pixies still remembered today in Ottery St Mary's Pixie Day. Of interest are the many initials carved in the cliff face, which included at one time those of Samuel Coleridge Taylor.

Mill Street, Ottery St Mary, c.1908, showing the mail cart outside the old post office.

Ottery St Mary & District Co-op. Seen here in around 1928, but certainly here since Victorian times, the shop in Yonder Street is still serving Ottery St Mary with its grocery needs.

Tip Hill, Ottery St Mary, c.1915.

The Half Moon Inn, North Street, Ottery St Mary (c.1890), which was later bought by the Sidmouth-based Vallance's Brewery, had the town's Pound (the door on the right) as its neighbour. The Pound was closed around 1932, but the Half Moon survived until the late 1970s and is now a private residence which still retains the stained-glass windows complete with their 'Bar' legends.

Batts Lane, Ottery St Mary, c.1906. The Baptist Chapel is on the left. Luxton's Inn is now the Lamb and Flag.

The King's Arms in Gold Street, seen here in around 1910 when it was owned by Mr Trickey, is said to be Ottery St Mary's oldest inn and was the coaching stop for the town. The shop just visible on the right was Harold Samson's greengrocery.

Fire at the corner of Rag Lane and North Street, Ottery St Mary, in 1905, during which six thatched cottages were destroyed. Although Rag Lane is officially part of North Street (and is numbered as such) to all Ottregians is has always been known as Rag Lane because, it is said, of the ragged clothes worn by the working-class people who lived here in former times.

The house at the corner of Rag Lane and North Street which replaced the left-hand cottage seen above. Ironically, it was severely damaged by fire in early 1994 and is still awaiting rebuilding.

Tanners Hill, Mill Street, Ottery St Mary, c.1960. The tannery (in the background) and the cottage were demolished in the 1980s and the site is now the entrance to Millcroft housing estate.

Silver Street, Ottery St Mary, c.1908. Slee's Bazaar, which doubled as a toy and family bazaar and a tobacconist, is now a Chinese take-away.

Building the King's School, 1912.

Sir John Kennaway laying the foundation stone of the new Ottery King's School. The school had been founded by Henry VIII as a free grammar school 'to endure always for all time to come,' its origins being the former choir school that vanished in the wake of the Dissolution. It declined considerably around 1850-1880. In 1883 it moved to The Priory, opposite the church, but moved again in 1912 to its present home at Thorne.

34

Two
Ottery St Mary
The People

Joan Palfrey, daughter of a well-known Ottery family, was employed as a nanny and is seen here in around 1935. Few, however, would argue with the statement that the star of the picture is the pram!

Ottery St Mary Infants School, May Day 1949. Back row, left to right: Baker, Annett Harris, -?-, Betty Parsons. Centre: Mansfield, Turner, Rosalind Streat, Pollard, -?-. Front: John Glanville, -?-.

Ottery St Mary Boys' School, Yonder Street, 1931-32. Back row, left to right: -?-, Gerald Retter, Steve Wheaton, Clive Retter, John Franks, Don Hadfield, Bill Johns, Vivien Verschoren, Miss Hooper. Third row: Don Dyer, ? Pike, Reg Shapter, Wilf Baker, ? Palfrey, Stan Bolt, ? Palfrey, Derek Heale, Granville Matthews. Second row: Archie Retter, Stanley Young, George Urquhart, Peter Arbury. Front: Brice Bending, Tony Cann, Tommy Tolman, Jeff Woodley, Mick Avery.

The Brock family also owned a general furnishing shop in Mill Street, seen here with Doris Selley (née Brock) in the door. Today Cut & Curl occupies the site.

Ottery St Mary British Legion (the 'Royal' came later) Fête Queen and attendants, 1943:
Barbara Oak, Ethel Carnell (queen), Elsie Kite.

Mr Hine with his family outside his bakery in Paternoster Row, Ottery St Mary, c.1914. The double door to the right led to the bakehouse.

Miss E.G. Goodlad, standing beside Revd Maitland Kelly, vicar of Ottery St Mary 1890-1900, lays the foundation stone at Ottery St Mary's Church Institute in Yonder Street on 5 September 1895. Miss Goodlad financed the building and, at one time, lived at Beaumont House, Ridgeway. The old girls' school (now flats) is in the background, and the cottage hospital on the extreme right skyline.

Ottery Town Band at The Land of Canaan, Ottery St Mary, c.1927. Standing, left to right: Ernest Reed, Stan Simons, -?-, Fred Baker (band master), George West. Seated: Harry Basten, Reg Berry, -?-, Albert Salter, -?-. Front: Ern Stuckey, Reg Eveleigh.

Retirement of District Nurse Loosemore at Ottery St Mary Church Institute in around 1958, when she was presented with a television set collected for by the people of the town. Left to right: Ernie Miles, Mrs Trail, Miss Mona Inglefield, Mr H.J. Inglefield, W.F. Bennett, Nurse Beatrice Loosemore, Dr R.R. Trail, Miss Rita Loosemore (back), Vera Ellis (who took over from Nurse Loosemore), -?-.

Ottery St Mary Volunteer Fire Brigade at the Land of Canaan in Ottery in August 1889. Back row, left to right: H. Gover, Tom Dyer (sen), Deputy Captain George Channon, Capt J.H. Newton, R. Banfield, E. 'Knocker' Stocker, C. Salter. Middle: J. Streat, C. Harding, G. Ford, G. Meldon, W. 'Betsy' Carter, Tom Dyer (jun). Front: R. Channon, W. Davis, Fred Stuckey. 'Knocker' Stocker owed his nickname to the fact that when there was a fire at night he went around knocking the firemen's windows with a long pole. During the day he blew a horn which was also used to warn pedestrians that the horse-drawn fire engine was on its way.

Ottery St Mary Fire Brigade 1950. Back row, left to right: Charles Turner, Frank Down, Tom Bishenden, Bill Berry. Front: Jack Rowland, Bill Manley, Charles Ash.

Ottery St Mary Volunteer Fire Brigade, which lost its 'Volunteer' adjective in 1913 when it came under the local council's control, is seen here in 1911 outside the Chanter's House. Back row, left to right: Fred Salter, Jimmy Cann, George Whitcombe, Jimmy Sparks. Front: George Prigg, Tommy Marker, Harry Stuckey, Sub Capt Frank Street, Capt Harry Channon, T. Parsons, George Dyer, Syd Baker (landlord of the Mason's Arms).

Ottery St Mary handbell ringers, in the garden of the vicarage, 1891.

Ottery St Mary handbell ringers at the rear of the Vicarage, c.1894. Ottery's vicar from 1890 to 1900, the Revd Maitland Kelly is on the right; the three young ladies are his daughters. John Godfrey is extreme left, Walter Godfrey on the girls' left.

Ottery St Mary handbell ringers, 1949. Left to right: Alan Gollop, Roy Doble, Frank Down, Jim Palfrey, Reg Marks, Nelson Owen.

Old Ottregians Day Annual Meeting in London, c.1908. Sidney Godfrey (secretary) is seated beside Lord Bernard Coleridge (President) centre front.

The consecration of the Church Army Van outside St Mary's church, Ottery St Mary, c.1901.

Crowd outside St Mary's church waiting for the arrival of Princess Alice of Teck and General Buller in 1909.

Empire Day in Broad Street, Ottery St Mary, 1909. Cannicott's (the drapers) is in the background.

Peace Thanksgiving in Ottery Square, 6 July 1919. Bovett's the bakers (later Harris) is in the background.

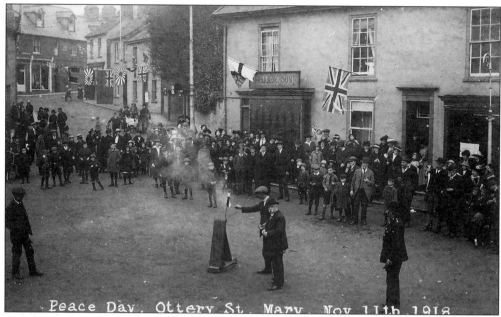

A maroon is let off in Ottery St Mary's Broad Street at 11am on 11 November 1918 to mark the cessation of hostilities in World War One.

Reg Harris (right, beside his 1939 1¼-litre MG in Broad Street, Ottery St Mary) moved to Ottery from Exmouth in 1941, when his bakery business was destroyed by bombing. He took over Bovett's Broad Street bakery soon afterwards, remaining in business there until 1960-61 when he retired. The premises were demolished and Baxter's (now Dewhurst's) butchers shop built in its place.

Ottery St Mary Girl Guides, c.1915.

Ottery St Mary Boy Scouts gathering moss during World War One. One of the troop's wartime activities was collecting moss from Pixies' Parlour, Head Weir, and surrounding woodlands. They then met the Red Cross trains at Sidmouth Junction. The moss was used for wound dressings. Among the scouts are Charles Turner and 'Ginger' Prigg.

The East Devon Hunt in Ottery St Mary Square, c.1908.

The choir of the Collegiate Church of St Mary's of Ottery, March 1871. Back row, left to right: W.J.S. Digby, G.S. Whitcombe, E. Carnell, F.D. Carnell, A.T. Warne, G. Streat, C. Gover, T.S. Digby. Front: G.T. Channon, G. Rendell, H. Streat, W. Wright, C.H. Whitcombe, J.S. Gover, L. Shorland, J. Pullman, J.W. Warne, F. Stuckey, E.R. Lippett. The organist is Mr T.J. Carnell.

Old Ottregian Mr Percival, who lived at Southernhay in Longdogs Lane, snapped walking along Mill Street in 1932.

St Mary's Church Choir, 1936. Back row, left to right: Charles Turner, Frank Richards, Mr Down (schoolmaster), Reg Oke, Arthur Prigg, Ron Clapp, Ken Gerry. Fourth row: Leo Lovell, Jack Arbury (sexton), George Bow, Jimmy Baker, Harry Westaway, Tommy Whicker, Henry Reed, Nelson Owen. Third row: Clifford Bending, Brice Bending, Frank Down, Donald Dyer, George Osborne (organist), Mr Dupe (lay reader), Revd L.B. Stallard (vicar), Revd Benjamin Crockett (curate), Norman Abrahams, Ron Gibbons, Derek Heale, Ken Arbury. Second row: Stanley Morcom, Victor Lovell, Jim Palfrey, Tony Cann, Arthur Isaac, Reg Morcom, Terry Edmond, David Loveless, Ron Salter, Benjamin Bolt. Front row: David Cann, Reg Bolt, Terry Loveless.

Arthur 'Ginger' Prigg, the baby in front, seen with members of his family outside their Sandhill Street home, c.1906.

Church of England Boys' School in Yonder Street, 1933. Back row, left to right: Fred Turner, Arthur Gigg, Vivien Verschoren, Bill Johns, Frank Down, Les Salter, Miss Hooper. Third row: Ron Gibbons, Derek Heale, Norman Drew, Archie Retter, Tony Cann, Peter Arbury, Joel Wonnacott, Peter Ayres. Second row: Gordon Sparks, Jeff Woodley, Fred Bending, Jim Palfrey, Sydney Willis, Owen Taylor, Gapper Whitwell. Front: Royce Luxton, -?-, Jack Retter, Ken Hawkins, Michael Avery, Brice Bending, Albert Isaac, Ernie Palfrey.

Mr A. Cripps, chief parade marshal for
Ottery St Mary Carnival, in 1907.

The post office staff and postmen at Ottery St Mary around 1890. George Ware is second left in
the back row.

Mrs Bessie Powlesland (grandmother of Mrs Ann Channon), who lived at Dunkirk, Hind Street, outside Ottery St Mary post office in Mill Street.

Billy Handford, seen here in 1932 in his fireman's sub-captain uniform, was one of the Ottery St Mary blacksmiths who served as a farrier during World War One. His forge in Yonder Street can be seen behind; today it is a coal depot.

Three

At Work ...

East Devon Motor Company, Mill Street, Ottery St Mary, 1927. The proprietor, Henry John Lee, is on the extreme right. Known today as Down's Motors, the premises have been considerably altered and rebuilt.

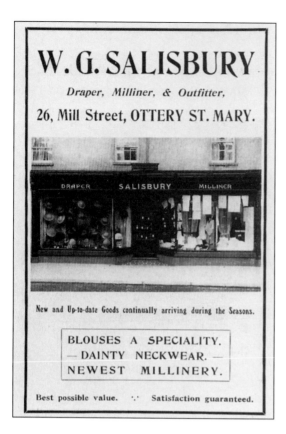

W.G. Salisbury, drapers and milliners at 26 Mill Street, Ottery St Mary, seen here in 1912. This became Chambers' drapers, then Mr L.C. Jones' grocery shop. (With those initials it will come as no surprise to learn that he was nicknamed 'Elsie'. Today the premises are a supermarket.

Foxenhole Mills, West Hill, c.1910. Eveleigh, the miller's, workers lived on the left, Eveleigh on the right; the mill was in the centre. This is now four houses.

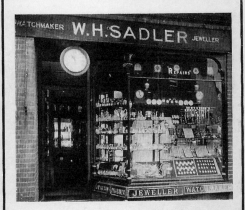

W. H. SADLER

Watchmaker, Jeweller, & Silversmith,

Silver St., OTTERY ST. MARY.

Silver, Plate, Gold and Gem Jewellery, Watches, Clocks, Silver Souvenir Spoons,
ETC.
Well-equipped workshop for all repairs.

W.H. Sadler's jewellers shop in Silver Street, Ottery St Mary, in 1912. This is today's Piper's Wine Shop.

Ottery St Mary cattle market in The Square, c.1905. The market, which was formerly held at The Flexton, moved to the town centre around the turn of the century and then moved to a site in Market Lane between the gas works and the saw mills around the time of World War One. The market closed as recently as the early 1960s.

Ottery St Mary station, c.1960.

On 30 June 1930 a steam-roller lost its front roller and crashed into a wall in Gold Street.

H. G. LUXTON, Wholesale & Retail Tobacconist.

General Sports Outfitter.

Stationer, Bookseller, Newsagent, :: and Fancy Goods Dealer. ::

China and Glass Warehouse.

| :: ORDERS TAKEN FOR :: WEDDING & MOURNING CARDS, :: RELIEF STAMPING, :: LETTERPRESS PRINTING, :: AND LITHOGRAPHY. :: | ROYAL DOULTON AND CROWN DEVON DINNER SETS, TEA SETS, TOILET WARE, &c. :: CREST AND VIEW CHINA. :: :: Agent for the Westminster Fire Office, Plate Glass Assurance Co., and The Commercial Union Assurance Co. PULLAR'S DYE WORKS, PERTH. |

Mill Street, OTTERY ST. MARY, Devon.

H.G. Luxton, in Ottery St Mary's Mill Street, was a stationer, bookseller, newsagent and tobacconist of some repute when this advertisment appeared in 1913. Still a newsagents, it now trades under the name of Eckett.

One of three Shand Mason manual hand-drawn pumps used by the Ottery St Mary UDC (formerly Volunteer) Fire Brigade with (left) a Merryweather hand hose-and-ladder cart. They are seen here in 1918 outside the fire station in Silver Street with Captain Harry Stuckey. The hose-and-ladder cart cost £27 17s. 9d. when purchased in 1913. It was lettered in gold vermillion and brought to the town by the L&SWR from London.

The Factory (Otter Mill Switch Gear) in around 1919, when it was Coleberd's bottling plant for Kop's Ale and Stout.

The mill leat, c.1910. This fed the water wheels at the Georgian serge factory. The pipe took waste water from Ottery's streets down to the River Otter.

The Mill Stream, seen here in the 1930s, fed the water wheels in both the corn mill and the serge factory which stood beside the Otter and now houses the Otter Mill Switchgear Ltd factory in Mill Street. Excess water was returned to the river by the 'tumbling' weir seen here and thought to be unique. Ottery's first elecricity was generated in Digby's old corn mill. The 110-volt DC dynamo was insufficient to meet winter demands and an anthracite-fired gas-driven Tangye engine in the adjacent factory was used to boost supply. That first electricity came courtesy of Mr Colberd, the factory owner, who was a great benefactor to the town and was, among other things, skipper of the paddle steamer *The Duchess of Devonshire* which plied along the Channel coast and called at nearby Seaton and Sidmouth. Colberd Hall in Tar Lane, off Mill Street, which later became the Drill Hall, is named after him.

Harry Connett, who lived at Gosford Lane, Escot, seen at the wheel of his steam-roller in around 1922. Connett, who worked for Devon County Council, spent the week living in a caravan that was towed behind the steam-roller. He is seen here with a local road gang.

An Ottery St Mary Devon County Council tar gang, c.1935. Harry Ebdon is known to be one member; Dick Eveleigh is fourth from left.

J.H. 'Jack' Prigg was an Ottery-based carrier whose adverts pointed out that he went to 'Exeter Tuesdays and Fridays' and that there was 'nothing too big, nothing too small'. He began business just after World War One with an ex-Army Albion, and is seen here after crashing into a double-decker bus in Exeter. The blackout discs on each vehicle's headlights and the white marks on the bus's front wings suggest that this picture was taken during World War Two. The lorry was often used as a 'bus' at weekends, regular customers being the Taleford Merry Makers Dance Band (and their supporters) who bumped along country lanes on Saturday evenings to village hops around Ottery.

Ottery St Mary Brickworks, c.1920. Back row only, left to right: John Woodley (sen), the manager John Woodley, -?-, Bob Woodley, -?-, Harry Piney, -?-. The men with the aprons made 'handmades' which were, as the name suggests, hand-made bricks baked in wooden moulds.

Staff at Ottery Brickworks, 1928. Left to right: John Woodley (manager), Mac Burnie, Mr Wallace, Jack Woodley, Bert Dunford, Mr Wallace, Walter Piney, Jack Piney, Mr Berry, Percy Welsford, -?-, Harry Hill, Harry Passey, Tommy Taylor (front), Bill Palfrey, Bill Thompson, Harry Piney, Harry Welsman, Albert Salter, -?-, Ivor Welsford.

The staff at Ottery St Mary Brickworks in 1959 on the occasion of John Woodley's retirement. Left to right: Harry Welsman, Bill Eveleigh, Fred Beer, Percy Welsford, Jock Osborne, Alf Matthews, Maurice Baker, Peter Jackson, Bill Tyrol, Jeff Woodley (manager), Mr Bending, Walter Piney, Jack Denham, George Totterdell, John Woodley (a former manager), Jim French, Jack Hartnell, Peter Baker, Mr Morris, Bert Windsor, Dennis Morgan, Jim Hudson, -?-, Charlie Lovering, Stan Chown, Fred Corrick, Bert Shears. Three generations of the Woodley family were works manager here: two Johns, and then Jeff, who still lives in the house, that once belonged to the brick company, in which he was born.

Salston Farm, c.1910, now a private mews.

Clay quarry at Ottery St Mary Brickworks, c.1936.

Four

... and Play

The East Devon Foxhounds meet at Salston on the occasion of the visit to the town of Prince and Princess Alexander of Teck in 1907.

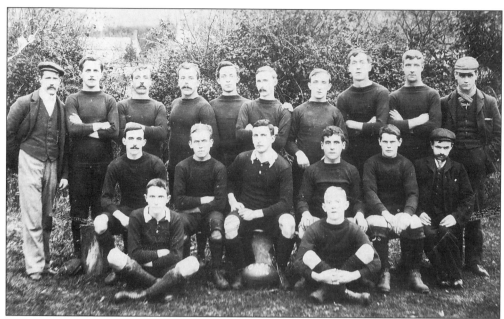

Ottery St Mary Rugby Club, 1906. A rugby club flourished in the town until 1913, when a switch was made to the association game, the rugby club's funds, assets and ground, which was then in a field beside the old Saw Mills and Market Place, being handed over to the new football club .

Ottery St Mary Football Club on their old ground beside the old Saw Mills in 1934. Back row, left to right: Fred Stuckey, Bert Maye, J. Bagwell, B. Boyland, J. North, G. Drawer. Front: R. Evans, Hector Stuckey, J. Hanson, B. Fowler, D. North.

Ottery St Mary Football Club, the side that beat Colyton 3-1 in a replay in the Seaton Supporters (now Seaton Challenge) Cup in 1952-53 after drawing the first game 1-1. Back row, left to right: Fred Turner, Eric Manning, Don Baker, -?-, Gordon Russell, 'Digger' Ebdon. Front: Dave Cann, Len Russell, Peter Spurway, Derek Heale, Roland Lovering.

Ottery St Mary Football Club, 1948-49. Back row, left to right: Hector Stuckey, Lionel Hele, Jimmy James, Ivor Tucker, Griffith, Woodley, Cleverton, Reg Eveleigh, Reed. Middle: Baker, Derek Hele, Pinney, Fred Turner, Marks, Ron Codling. Front: Les Dolling, Roy Isaac, John Bluck, Eric Manning, Jack Osborne.

Ottery St Mary Cricket Club, 1958. Left to right: F. Burns, J. Mewse, P. Bond, D. Finnegan, S. Baker, J. Harvey, J. Retter, H. Lawrence, C. Lamb, R. Pollard, L. Spencer, H. Channon, E. Whitcombe, R. Stone, W. Down. The occasion was the centenary of cricket in the town, games having been recorded since 1858. But it is highly unlikely that they were played by a body as organised as today's much-respected club, which regularly fields two teams in the local Exeter Bank (formerly Fox's) East Devon Cricket League and also plays a major role in fostering youth cricket. The game was first played at Cadhay, then on a pitch in the grounds of Salston House. The club is thought to have moved to its present home off Strawberry Lane, which was at one time part of the playing fields of the nearby Ottery King's School, as long ago as the early 1920s.

Ottery St Mary cricket field, 1950. Left to right: W. Westlake, H. Stuckey, R. Eveleigh, -?-, H. Carne.

Ottery St Mary Cricket Club annual dinner, 1950. Among members present are Jack Powlesland, Terry Wood, Harry Channon, Alan Down, Raymond Isaac, Revd Rufus Price, Ivor Tucker, Arthur Golesworthy and Cis Manley.

The Ottery & District Football League catered mainly for village sides in the area – and catered for them very well, the league enjoying a reputation second to none for its family atmosphere. Here members are gathered after an AGM at the Volunteer Inn in around 1950. Those present include Geoff Blackmore (now President of the Golesworthy Cup), Jack Selway (league secretary), Les Lazell (Awliscombe FC), Gilbert Burrough (Broadhembury FC) and Arthur Golesworthy (league chairman, later President).

Although this is a Sidford (Rodfords) outing at Cheddar in around 1924, it is Reg Summers (the driver) and his Mill Street, Ottery St Mary-based charabanc who have taken them there.

Although the occasion is not known, it is in around 1950 and has both WI and National Savings connections. Ted Dyer is driving the tractor and has Mrs Lovell among his passengers. The two girls among the spectators on the left are the Tucker sisters.

Ottery St Mary Carnival. Rock cannons, which were made locally at the Otter Mill factory and fired with gun powder normally used for blasting in local quarries, were part and parcel of the carnival but their origins are lost in the mists of time. For obvious reasons, the practice was stopped during World War Two and, judging by the posters, restarted eighteen years later, which dates this picture to 1956. Left to right: Alec Abbot, Eddie Whitcombe, Bastin, Peter Bull, Jimmy Isaac, Harry Channon, Nelson Owen, John Martin, -?-, Jim Pearcey.

The head of the Territorial Sunday Church Parade (November 1912) coming out of Mill Street into the Square. The (VAD?) nurses are lined up outside Bovett's (later Harris's) bakers shop. Caldicott, the draper and outfitters on the left, seems to have anticipated the large crowd and covered the shop windows.

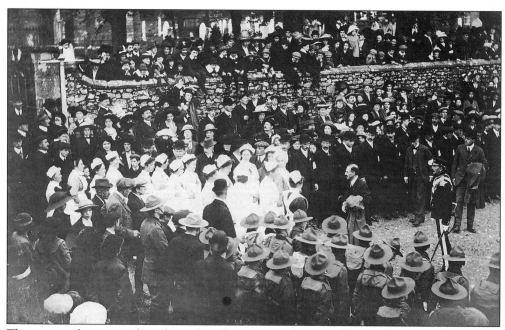

The nurses, who seem to have been thought too genteel to actually march, are now outside the church gates and, along with the Boy Scouts, are about to be inspected.

The Parade was important enough to have brought Sir John Kennaway out; he can be seen (with white beard) facing the officer.

The Territorial Sunday Church Parade moving through Ottery Square moving through Ottery Square, via Silver Street, and heading for St Mary's church.

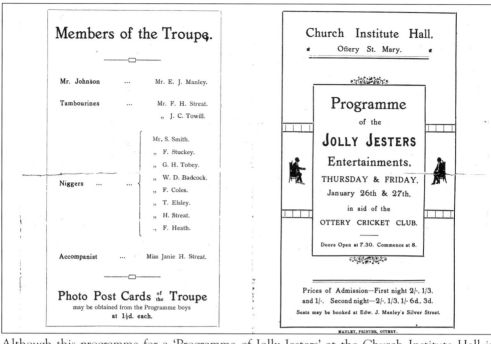

Although this programme for a 'Programme of Jolly Jesters' at the Church Institute Hall in Ottery St Mary in aid of Ottery Cricket Club does include a 'Musical Monologue 1950 by Mr W.D. Badcock' towards the bottom, its 1½d price for postcards of the Troupe, plus the names of many of the members, suggest that this is a printing error. It is most likely from the 1930s. The Campaign for Racial Equality would probably not be amused by some of the language but this was, after all, a vastly different age.

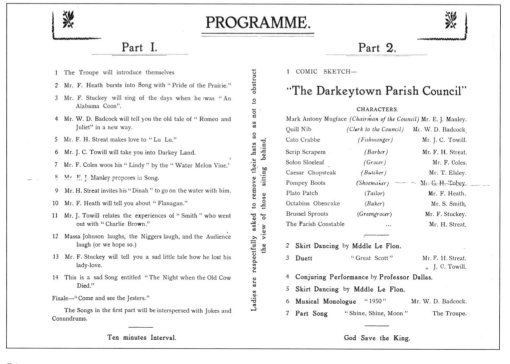

Ottery St Mary King's School hockey team, 1919-20. Zoe Godfrey is on Mr F. Wyatt, the headmaster's, left; Miss Andrews (headmistress) is on his right.

Ottery King's School 1st rugby XV, pictured at Tiverton, 1960. The Ottery players (darker shirts on the right) are, back row, left to right: Graham Price, Rodney Pidgeon, Williams, Bob Salway, Mike Gill, Dave Easterbrook, Andy Mills. Front: Bob Chambers, Martin Peaccock, Mike Huxtable (capt), Fred Farmer, Richard Palfrey, Roger Smallshaw, Roger Bagwell, -?-.

Culmstock Otter Hounds at Cadhay Bridge, 5 May 1913.

An unknown occasion (probably connected with Pixie Day) in Ottery Square in the 1950s. Revd Rufus Price (vicar 1950-78) is on the left; the ladies, left to right, are Ruby Turner, Violet Wood, Miss Hine, Mrs Glanville and Polly Marks. The fireman in the background is Charlie Ash.

An Ottery St Mary outing (c.1925) to an unknown destination and, most likely, in a coach belong to Dagworthy of Sidmouth. Among passengers are George Totterdell, Ed Bastin, Fred Palfrey, Sam Budd and Mr Heale, the Ottery blacksmith.

Masons Arms' outing, c.1951. Back row, left to right: Ern Stuckey, Bill Berry, George 'Jago' Welsman, George Isaacs, Jack Clitheroe (?), Tom Baker, 'Soldier' Berry, George Cann. Middle: Bill Palfrey, Syd Budd, Syd Salter, Greenaway, Sparks, 'Ginger' Howe, Syd Wills. Front: Jimmy James, Albert Hellier, Jack Loveless, Ernie Howe, Jack Woodley, Harry Piney, Buller Cann (landlord), Roy Isaacs, Ernie Baker.

Ottery outing to Bristol Zoo, c.1954. Mr Reg Harris, Mrs Harris, Milly Loveless, Maude Loveless, Mrs Reed, Annett Harris, Mrs Hurford, Mary Heal, Stan Symonds, 'Ginger' Leach, Reg Summers, Mr and Mrs Palfrey.

Ottery St Mary bell ringers outing to Cheddar, c.1924. There was a resident photographer at Gough's Cave in Cheddar who did a roaring business with charabanc outings. There can hardly be a town in the Devon that does not have a picture similar to this. The driver, Fred Lovering, was employed by Reg Summers, who had a garage in Mill Street. Garth Chapple, headmaster of the Boys' School, is standing behind.

Ottery Day, held annually on Whit Monday, was when ex-pat Ottregians living in London returned home. Their specially chartered trains from Waterloo were met at Ottery station by the Town Band and they were marched to the Church Institute for breakfast (the train having left London at around 4.00am). The rest of the day was spent in sports in the grounds of the Chanter's House and, after tea, members left for London to the strains of the band. The Godfrey family, who were boot makers in Silver Street, played a leading role in organising Ottery Day, and a member of that family is seen here in 1909 greeting the visitors outside Hellier & Son's butchers shop in the Square. The last Ottery Day was in 1914, the event not being restarted after World War One.

Ottery Day, 1909. Horse and traps from Lake's Livery Stables met people arriving by train for the long-awaited event.

Ottery Day in Silver Street, 1909. The first Ottery Day was held in 1907. It was quite common for around 1,000 members of the Old Ottregian Society to make the journey back to the town.

Ottery St Mary Old Comrades' Concert
Party, c.1923. W. Streat, ? Gregory, Fred
Stuckey, ? Pulman, Jim Arbury, Bill Badcock,
F. Law.

The Grand Templar of the Independent Order of Grand Templars entering Ottery St Mary via
Broad Street on his farewell tour of the West Country in around 1908.

The Handkerchief Bazaar of 20 December 1923 of Capt (Mrs) Evans' Salvation Army.

Ottery St Mary Carnival Pram Race, c.1955. The entrants, who had to down a drink at the eight pubs on the course, the Five Bells, Volunteer, London Hotel, King's Arms, Half Moon, Lamb & Flag, Mason's Arms and Plume of Feathers, are, left to right and passenger first: Gerald Woodley and Paul Vicary, Peter Bull and Eddie Whitcombe, Tony Bastin and Nelson Owen, Harold Lovering and Tom Croydon, Peter Harris and Bert Horrell and John Paddon and David Ash.

The North Street and Paternoster Row party at Ridgeway House, Dr Trail's residence, on 13 July 1951 during Ottery St Mary's Festival of Britain celebrations.

Ottery St Mary Town Band, c.1908.

Coronation celebrations outside the Mason's Arms in Sandhill Street in 1937.

Coronation celebrations in Yonder Street in 1937. The corner of the Church Institute is on the extreme left. Alan Dyer is the boy with the bicycle.

Coronation celebrations in Mill Street in 1937.

Silver Jubilee celebrations in The Square, Ottery St Mary, in 1935.

Pixie Day, Ottery St Mary, in the early 1950s.

Ottery St Mary Comrades' first outing on 10 June 1939. They include Bill Luxton, Jack Drew, Billy Hansford, Neddy Snell, Bill Berry, Reg Bridle, Syd Salter, Bert Ridge, Fred Bastyn, Reg Eveleigh, Ron Clapp, the Corrick twins Fred and Frank, Bill Palfrey, Ern Reed, F. Williams, Harry Stuckey, Mr Heale (Ottery's blacksmith), and Mr H. Smerdon (a local baker). The three men in the coach are Les Salter, Bill Corrick and Les Dolling.

Five

Whimple, Escot, Alfington and Feniton

Chelsea Farm, Feniton, c.1920.

Alfington, c.1912. The Alfington Inn still stands, but the attractive thatched house to its right has been demolished.

Alfington village, looking towards Ottery St Mary, c.1908. The trees and hedge on the left were removed in road widening schemes. Higher Woodford Farm, previously roofed with galvanised sheets, has recently been re-roofed with slate.

Escot Club Day, 1913. Ed Bastin of the Ottery St Mary Band is among those present.

Sir John Kennaway's sawmills at his Escot estate in 1908. Escot House itself was originally built in 1685 for Sir Walter Yonge of Colyton. During its construction, some of the workers are said to have downed tools and made off to join Monmouth's ill-fated rebellion. Those who survived Sedgemoor were captured and taken to Exeter, and then brought back to Talaton to be hanged and left on a gibbet at the crossroads to the east of the village, known ever since as Bittery Cross.

Escot's old village hall at Coombelake in 1953. The much-used hub of the tiny hamlet's social life was pulled down in the 1970s.

Escot Vicarage, seen here in around 1926, was burnt down in the 1960s and rebuilt as a private house. Escot's little church of St Philip and St John was built in its attractive Early English style with a bell-turrett by Sir John Kennaway in the mid-nineteenth century. Two years after the church was completed, Escot became a separate parish.

PROGRAMME.

Leave	Escot Village Club	...	7.45 a.m.
Arrive	Ilminster	... ...	9 a.m.
Leave	,,	... ...	9.30 a.m.
Arrive	Glastonbury ...	...	10.45 a.m.
Leave	,,	... ...	11.15 a.m.
Arrive	Wells	... ...	11.30 a.m.
Leave	,,	.. ...	1 p.m.
Arrive	Cheddar	... ...	2 p.m.
Leave	,,	.. ...	3 p.m.
Arrive	Weston-Super-Mare	...	4 p.m.
Leave	,, ,,	...	4.30 p.m.

RETURN.

Arrive	Bridgwater	.. ...	5.30 p.m.
Leave	,,	... ...	6.15 p.m.
Arrive	Taunton	... ...	7 p.m.
Leave	,,	... ...	7.45 p.m.
Arrive	Upottery	... ...	8.45 p.m.
Leave	,,	... ...	9 p.m.
Arrive	Fairmile	...	10 p.m.

RULES.—Any person or persons not being at the starting places at the times stated on the Programme will be left behind, the same would have to pay their own expenses to catch up the Char-a-banc or return home.

The Committee will not be responsible for any expenses caused by any person or persons at any time or place of the journey.

E. T. BASTIN, Hon. Sec., E.V.C.

Escot Club Outing card. Charabanc trips were long-awaited events and talked about for weeks after. But few villages could have planned theirs with as much military precision as Escot Outing Club. And how tired (but happy) must have been the villagers when, after a 7.45am start and a trek across half Devon and Somerset, they finally arrived back at the Fairmile Inn just before 'closing time'.

An Escot Outing at Gough's Cave, Cheddar, around 1924, where a resident photographer did a roaring trade with the day trippers. Fred Lovering is driving Reg Summers' charabanc, among his passengers are Edward Bastin, Alf Cummings and Bill Pearcy.

Coursing at Fairmile, c.1910.

Fairmile Inn, c.1906, then with the post office on its left. The name probably comes from a nearby and better ('faire') mile-long stretch of the old London–Exeter coaching road. Another suggestion is that the inn (and district) is 'a fair mile from Ottery'. A more entertaining, if less likely story has Oliver Cromwell, on his visit to Ottery, chasing a local Cavalier. The pursuit, it is said, lasted as far as the inn, where the fugitive collapsed crying out, 'I've led you a fair mile.' Fairmile Inn was there in the sixteenth century and became the coach stopping point for Ottery.

Sir John Kennaway presents a 1953 Coronation souvenier to his own daughter Marigold at Escot House.

Coombelake Corner, Escot. Mrs Vera Bastin is outside a house decorated for the 1953 Coronation.

The torch carrying the 1948 Olympic Flame on its last leg, from Plymouth to London, was taken along the A30 by local runners. Here the torch is handed over between members of Tiverton Athletic Club at Bellbottom, just above Fairmile towards Exeter. Locals watching include Jack Coles (extreme left), Dennis Bastin (boy below the torches), Jack Morman and Bill Berry (at back) and Cynthia Street (now Russell).

Escot School, c.1906.

The Fairmile Inn, c.1918.

Fairmile, c.1915, looking towards Honiton. The house on the left went in (A30) road widening schemes; the vicarage in the left background burnt down.

Escot Rovers Football Club, 1922-23.

Bill Sweetland's Mill, Fenny Bridges, c.1905. It was near the mill in 1549, in a field called Fenny Mead, that the Prayer Book Rebellion as good as ended when Lord Russell defeated an army of Devon and Cornish men up in arms against the imposition of the new prayer book. Both Feniton Manor House, which harboured the wounded, and the nearby Greyhound Inn, where the losers had made merry before the fight, were burnt to the ground in reprisal.

The old shop at Sandy Knapp, Feniton, c.1946, now a private residence with the lean-to and other left-hand parts enlarged and garages added.

The Greyhound Hotel at Fenny Bridges, on the A30 section of the London–Lands Ends trunk road, seen here in around 1929, took its name from the Greyhound coach that called there during the coaching era. The handsome bus on the right bears the name Pleesway.

Feniton Football Club, c.1950. Back row, left to right: Jim Connett, -?-, Bishop, Tony Carnall, John Virgin, -?-, Les Stevens, -?-. Front: -?-, -?-, -?-, -?-, -?-, Len Down.

Feniton Court, c.1920. The late Georgian building was the birthplace of John Coleridge Patteson (1827-71), the first missionary-bishop of Melanesia, who was murdered by natives at Santa Cruz.

Feniton, c.1921. The railings in front of the houses went in salvage drives during World War Two but have been replaced. Note that the signpost says Sidmouth Junction (and not Feniton station).

Curscombe Road, Feniton, c.1910. The extensions to the school house (right centre) were added in 1909.

Cursombe Road, Feniton, looking the opposite way to the picture on the opposite page, c.1910. Home Farm is on the right.

Adder's (formerly Addle) Hole, Feniton, c.1920. Adder's Hole, the centre building, was once a Poor House; Chown's workshop, beyond it, used to be a butchers shop.

The Hand and Pen Inn opposite the Whimple turning on the A30 road, seen here in around 1930, was later was converted into houses.

Wayside Café, on the A30 between Whimple and Ottery St Mary, now the Wayside Country Restaurant. This opened for Whit Weekend 1926, when it was the pioneer in roadside eating establishments, the only one between Salisbury and Exeter. It cost a local farmer, who was struggling to cope financially, £146 to build. Before the war it was visited by several celebrities, including Prince Olaf of Norway on his honeymoon in May 1929. Signing the visitor's book incognito, he wrote that he had just had his first Devon cream tea. The Marchioness of Queensbury was so taken with the cuisine on offer that she had a weekly order of creams and eggs for several years.

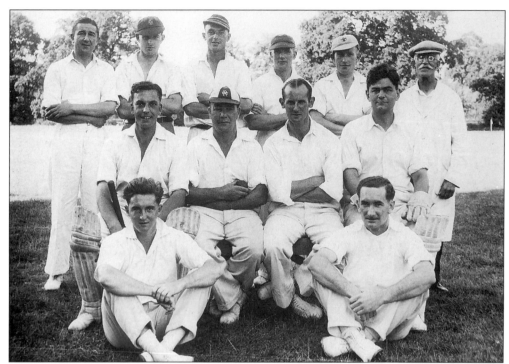

Whimple & Whiteways Cricket Club, 1947. Back row, left to right: G. Stanines, H. Breyley, E. Smith, W. Hurved, R. Hartnoll, C. Baxter, E. Knight. Middle: G. Hurved, H. Mallett (capt), R. Whiteway (vice capt). Front: K. Grant, D. Watts.

Whimple & Whiteways Cricket Club, 1927. Back row, left to right: Harver, Clear, Hamilton, Huggins, Rose, James. Front: Davey, Atkinson, Norrish (capt), Snell, Hamilton.

Whimple & Whiteways Football Club, 1946-47, the season the team finished third in Junior 1 in the Exeter & East Devon League. Back row, left to right: T. Perry, R. Mahers, D. Roach, W. Potter, E. Smith, J. Scott. Front: W. Roach, D. Watts, S. Harris, L. Wheaton (capt), J. Hansford, F. Bess.

Station Road, Whimple, c.1910. Apart from the porches of the houses on the left, little has changed in the view from almost underneath the railway bridge. The entrance to Grove Road is in the left foreground.

The 1st Whimple Boy Scout Troop enjoy tea at Larkbeare House on 13 July 1911.

The first Ford automobile in Whimple, seen here in The Square in around 1909, was owned by local shopkeeper Mr Read, who earnt his 'Lippy' nickname after obtaining several crates of Lipton's tea at the outbreak of World War One. This is said to have netted him a small fortune later on when tea was rationed.

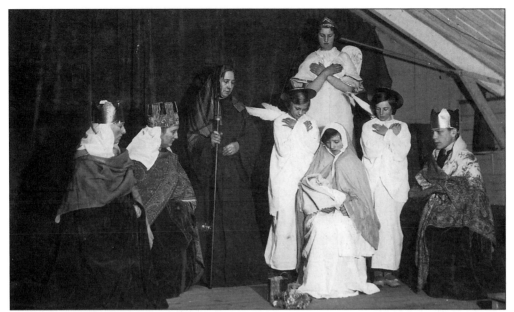

A Nativity Play in Whimple's Victory Hall, c.1924. Mrs Mullins, Mrs Fragal and Mrs G. Dart are on the left; the others are Queenie Wheaton, Lucy Caswell, Pam Sweetland, Rhoda Wood and Arthur Perry.

A choral occasion in Whimple's Victory Hall in around 1925. Among those present are: Alan Carthew, Jack Oxford, Arthur Retter, Dennis Watts, Derek and Richard Webber, Bert Hutchings, Frank Colman and Ted Brown.

Town Lane and The Green, Whimple, c.1910, with Robert Shepherd on the bridge. The right-hand side of Town Lane has been much developed today and there is now one house on the left-hand side as well.

Read's Stores, The Square, Whimple, c.1912. Mr Read, who was an amateur radio enthusiast (note the tall aerial), produced and sold many of the Whimple postcards in this section.

The ancient custom of wassailing, as seen here at Rull Farm, Whimple in around 1932, was revived in the village in 1993. There must be something in it – in 1994 there was a record amount of apple blossom. Mr and Mrs Jimmy Reynolds, who farmed Rull, are the couple immediately to the right of the wassail jug.

Whimple railway station, c.1908.

Empire Day 1906 in Whimple Square.

The New Inn, Whimple, seen here in around 1910, changed its name to the Thirsty Farmer some ten or twelve years ago.

Miss Flora Harris outside Rose Cottage, The Green, Whimple, 1905. She later became Mrs James Shepherd, the wife of a local thatcher.

The distribution of Coronation mugs by Lady Hughes of Larkbeare House outside St Mary's church, Whimple. Although the card is marked 1936 on both front and back, surely this is 1937 and the coronation of George VI? In contrast to the boys, most of whom are capless, the little girls are all wearing their best hats.

A choir outing to Gough's Cave at Cheddar, where the resident photographer did a roaring trade with charabanc outings. This is most likely local man Tom Turl's vehicle. Whimple's blacksmith Bertie Kenwood is thought to be the man next to the driver; next to him is thought to be Richard Webber.

This cottage in Whimple's Square, seen here in around 1908, later became Grant's bakery business. Today it is the Art Shop.

Whimple's 'Guildhall' in Church Road, seen here after a disastrous fire in November 1909, owed its nickname to the fact that one of the village's mock mayors lived there for many years.

The post office and the Police Station, Whimple, c.1934. Today the post office has moved to beside St Mary's church and the village no longer has a police station.

Whimple Reading Room, with St Mary's church in the background, c.1903. The church was rebuilt in 1845 and only the low tower survived of the original building, which was just as well as its stunted pinnacles are unusual and distinctive. Thomas Heberden was vicar here for fifty-seven years.

Whimple, c.1905.

Whimple School (now a private house), c.1910.

Slewton House, Whimple, c.1906.

The Green, Whimple. Seen here in around 1904, the attractive village centre has hardly changed in ninety years.

Whimple, c.1906.

114

Six
Newton Poppleford and Tipton St John

Exeter Inn, Newton Poppleford, c.1920.

Cannon Inn, Newton Poppleford, c.1905. Note the stables on the left.

The Post Office and Stores, Newton Poppleford, c.1909. Note the telegram sign.

Newton Poppleford, c.1919. Taken at the bottom of the village this picture shows the Oak Tree Garage on the left.

Bridge End, Newton Poppleford, c 1914. The road, now the A3052, has, of course, been widened. Bridge End, later a popular tea and guest house, was burnt down in the late 1980s and has just been rebuilt.

Newton Poppleford Football Club in 1947-48, when they were Ottery & District League champions. Back row, left to right: P. Retter, M. Flowers, R. Evans, J. Curtis, -?-, F. Stone, G. Hitchcock, -?-. Front: B. Clements, R. Stone, -?-, P. Spurway, R. Spurway.

Bridge End, Newton Poppleford, c.1952. Among the more interesting of Devon's place names, Newton Poppleford derives from two separate periods. The 'Popple' ford part, from 'the ford by the pebbles' (round stones known as 'Budleigh pobbles' are found locally) is Old English or Saxon; 'new ton' refers to a now-unknown and probably post-Norman settlement close at hand.

The Exeter Inn, c.1900. This popular coaching inn on the A5052 (formerly A35) is still very much a part of Newton Poppleford's social life.

Newton Poppleford, c.1906. The open space in front of St Luke's church is now built on. St Luke's was once a chantry of the church of the Blessed Virgin Mary at Aylesbeare, but was separated in 1862.

The lower end of Newton Poppleford village, c.1906. The oak tree on the right has long since gone, but it gives it name to the modern Oak Tree Garage, which stands back from today's much-improved main road.

Newton Poppleford School, c.1919. Back row, left to right: Frank Bridle, Cyril Hayman, George Holland, Victor West, Dick Carter, Charlie Parkhouse. Middle: Bill Podbury, Albert Mitchell, Gwen Lethbridge, Phyllis Radford, Bessie Marchant, May Howe, Lizzie Quaintance, Bill Drake. Front: Daisy Retter, Bessie Perry, Joan Carter, Gertie Faytor, Frances Roberts, Winnie Spurway.

Tipton St John, c.1906, looking towards the Sidmouth Road.

Tipton St John, c.1910, looking west towards the level crossing. Tipton takes its name from 'Tippa's' (an Old English personal name) ton or farm. The St John, which refers to the local church's dedication, came much later.

Flood damage at Tipton St John post office in 1909.

Tipton St John post office after its move in 1909 when the original office was destroyed by floods.

Tipton St John Football Club, c.1950. Back row, left to right: T. May, J. Sargent, J. Crockford, T. Parsons, T. Andrews, T. Horne, E. Sargent. Front: R. Manley, C. Ralls, J. Fowler, T. Ralls, F.Pike.

Tipton St John School, c.1950.

Tipton St John station and level crossing, c.1931. The filling station on the right is now a modernised garage run by Mr Richard Miles.

Golden Lion, Tipton St John, c.1906. The shop on the opposite side of the road is now the village post office.

Tipton St John Sports, 1912. The interesting thing here is the station in the background and the volume of goods traffic on view, proof indeed that our forefathers really did use the trains. BR may fail to get right which type of snowflake to hope for, but the old Southern Railway Company, which operated the branch line, persisted in putting Tipton St Johns on the station's name board.

Tipton St John station, c.1900, Mr Dart the stationmaster has goods ready for the next train. (Note the rabbits.) The Sidmouth branch line was opened on 6 July 1874 with intermediate stations at Ottery St Mary and Tipton St John; the Budleigh Salterton branch, which was extended to Exmouth from Tipton St John in 1903, opened on 15 May 1897. Both lines were closed to passenger traffic on 6 March 1967.

West Hill, c.1920. The car repairs business is now Potter's Country Market (see below).

The post office, West Hill, c.1906. Combined here with Potter's Shoeing and General Blacksmiths business, the site is today Potter's Country Market, which incorporates the post office into the supermarket and hairdressing side of the business.

Wiggaton, c.1905. Situated on the Sidmouth road, just to the south of Ottery St Mary, Wiggaton is still a place for the motorist to pass through with caution. It takes its attractive name from 'wicgincland' (Wicga's farm and land) on an old thirteenth-century document.

The AA sign at Wiggaton hamlet just outside Ottery St Mary. The first of these once-famous signs was placed at Hatfield, Herts in 1906, and by the 1930s there were over 40,000 of them in England. They were taken down in 1940 during World War Two invasion scares (it wouldn't do for the Germans to know where they were!) and very few survived to be returned to their old homes after 1946. Today only 100, including this one, are thought to remain. Obvious collector's items, they fetch £100 each.

Ottery King's School, 1922. The school was founded in 1545 by Henry VIII. It was re-organised in 1895 after being closed for six years. In 1911 it was re-constituted as a co-educational school under the Devon County Council. The school moved to its present home in 1912.

Acknowledgements

We are deep in debt to Frank Down, not only for his excellent introduction and many of the pictures to be found in this book, but for kindly reading the typescript and supplying a great deal of information; his love for his native town is much in evidence. Along with Frank, the following have kindly made pictures available to us: Sheila Baker, Ann and Harry Channon, Joan and Alan Dyer, Henry Godfrey, Mike Huxtable, John Lovell and Ottery St Mary Cricket Club, Mell and Babs Mead, Mr and Mrs Ron Prettyjohn, Pam Prigg, John Shepherd of the Whimple History Society, Roger Smith and Whimple Cricket Club, Carol and Bob Tanner, George Tenney, Trevor Vanstone of the *Sidmouth Herald*, Ottery St Mary's as well as Sidmouth's local paper, and Jeff Woodley. Our thanks to them all.

We must also thank our wives for putting up with the disruptions to their normally orderly households; especially Pat for the ever ready cuppa.